**Membri della commissione
internazionale di selezione
1987
(da sinistra a destra)**

**Members of the 1987
international selection
committee
(from left to right)**

*Tomio Yoshioka
Kodansha
Tokyo
Japan*

*Andreu Teixidor de Ventos
Ediciones Destino
Barcelona
Spain*

*David Grant
Hodder & Stoughton
London
Great Britain*

*Michael Neugebauer
Neugebauer Press
Salzburg, München
Austria*

*Arthur Hubschmid
L'Ecole des loisirs
Paris
France*

La Commissione di selezione 1987 ha esaminato le opere di 618 illustratori, alcuni affermati, altri esordienti, giungendo a una scelta finale di 88 artisti da 27 paesi. 14 gli illustratori inclusi nella mostra e nel catalogo per giudizio unanime e immediato da parte dei membri della giuria; gli altri sono stati selezionati con i voti della maggioranza.

I principali criteri adottati per la selezione sono stati l'originalità delle opere, la loro qualità artistica e tecnica, l'impatto sul ragazzo, la capacità innovativa e la varietà stilistica. Si è rilevato come tutti gli artisti selezionati e non ancora pubblicati mostrino un potenziale valido per la pubblicazione, pur nella diversità degli stili e linee di racconto a seconda dei diversi paesi del mondo.

È stato manifestato rincrescimento per il fatto che moltissimi artisti di fama internazionale non avessero presentato le loro opere, come pure per la quasi totale assenza di illustrazioni cosiddette «commerciali», quali i fumetti.

Inoltre è stato sottolineato con un certo disappunto che una gran parte delle opere candidate mancavano di apertura e di provocatorietà e non riflettevano adeguatamente la realtà in cui si muovono i ragazzi d'oggi.

I membri della commissione si sono comunque compiaciuti per la larga presenza di nuovi talenti e hanno espresso l'augurio che negli anni futuri artisti sempre più numerosi sottopongano alla selezione le loro creazioni.

The jury looked at works submitted by 618 illustrators, some established, others so far unpublished. They reduced the number finally to 88 from 27 countries.

There was immediate and total agreement about the inclusion in the exhibition and catalogue of 14 artists. The others were selected for inclusion by a majority vote, the principal criteria being originality, artistic and technical merit, child appeal, innovation and overall variety of style.

The jury took the view that all of the selected artists, who have not yet been published, display a publishable quality, recognizing that different styles and storylines appeal more or less in different countries of the world.

The jury regretted that most established artists had not submitted examples of their work, and noted the almost total absence of most «commercial» work, for example comic strips, among the submissions. The jury also voiced some disappointment that so much of the work was restrained and unchallanging and did not better reflect the real world in which children live.

However, the jury members were encouraged by a display of new talent and hope that in future years even more artists and their potential publishers will offer work for selection.

Elenco illustratori ammessi in ordine alfabetico

Alphabetical list of selected illustrators

Paesi di provenienza

Countries of origin

Algeria
Argentina
Australia
Austria
Belgium
Bulgaria
Canada
Cuba
Czechoslovakia
Denmark
Federal Republic of Germany
Finland
France
Great Britain
Iran
Italy
Japan
Netherlands
New Zealand
Poland
Portugal
Spain
Switzerland
Turkey
Uruguay
USA
USSR

ANNUAL '87

Pamela Allen

Address
109 Broughtow Street
Milsons Point, Sydney 2061 NSW
(Australia)

Place and date of birth
Auckland (New Zealand),
3 April 1934

Art School attended
Elam School of Art, Auckland

Works published by
Hamish Hamilton/London
The Bodley Head/London
Collins Australia/Sydney
Thomas Nelson
Australia/Melbourne
Librairie Flammarion/Paris
Lothrop/New York
Coward, McCann/New York
Geohegan/New York
Putnam/New York
Hodder & Stoughton/New Zealand

Title of the work
A Lion in the Night

Publisher and date of publication
Thomas Nelson/Flammarion
Hamish Hamilton/Carlsen/
Hodder & Stoughton, 1985
Putnam, 1986

Technique
Ink, watercolour, pen and brush

She saw a lion stealing the baby
Out of the castle and over the fields
Out of the forest and past the church
Into the boat and across the sea
Over the mountain and into the
fields

Maria Ida Amadei

Address
Via Schievano 12
20137 Milano (Italy)

Place and date of birth
Bologna, 8 April 1941

Art School attended
Art Institute, Bologna

Title of the work
The Game of the Goose

Technique
Etching

To catch her he acted cunningly
He caught her in bewilderment
«Leave!» he shouted
«Here, I've caught you!». The goose's
heart was beating madly

Françoise Amadieu

Address
19bis Rue de Verdun
91120 Palaiseau (France)

Place and date of birth
Pau, 15 July 1948

Art School attended
School of Fine Arts

Works published by
Editions Milan / Toulouse
Editions Nathan / Paris
Hachette / Paris
Editions Lito / Champigny s / M
Editions de l'Agora / Geneva

Title of the work
Seagull in Paris

Technique
Ink, air brush

Prison
«Folies Bergères»

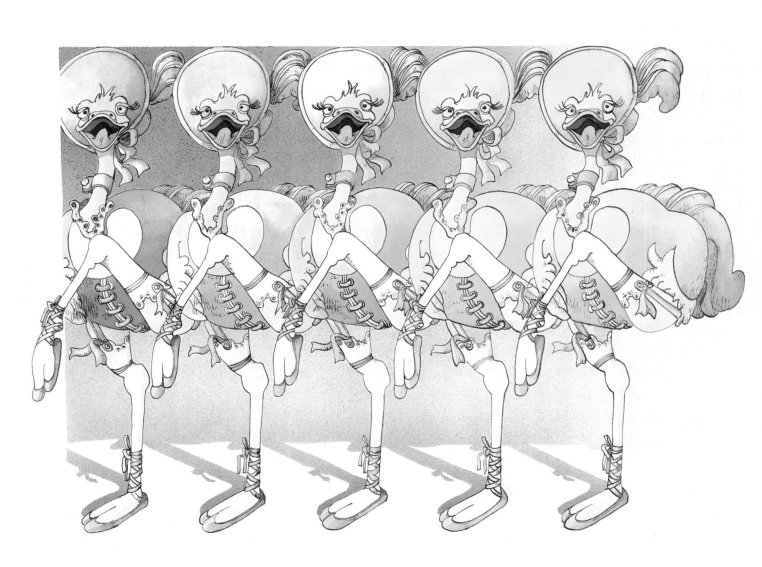

Martha Balaguer

Address
C/Sant Rafel 21c
Sant Cugat del Vallès-Barcelona
(Spain)

Place and date of birth
Barcelona, 19 April 1953

Works published by
Ediciones Destino/Barcelona
L'Abadia de Montserrat/Barcelona
Ediciones La Galera/Barcelona

Title of the work
Book of the «Voliches»,
«Laquidamios» and Other Kinds of
People

Publisher and date of publication
Ediciones Destino, 1986

Technique
Ink, watercolour

The «Laquidamios»

Barbara and Gerd Baumann

Address
Freudental 5
6060 Schwebisch Gmünd
(Federal Republic of Germany)

Dates of birth
14 August 1951
16 November 1950

Art School attended
Institute for Figurative Arts,
Schwäbisch Gmünd

Title of the work
Alphazet Book

The letter A for ant
The letter C for clown
The letter H for house
The letter L for loop
The letter M for meter

Tomasz Bogacki

Address
Nowowiejska 6/31
00 649 Warszawa (Poland)

Place and date of birth
Konin, 1 April 1950

Art School attended
Academy of Fine Arts, Warsaw

Works published by
Krajowa Agencja
Wydawnicza/Warsaw

Title of the work
Sleeping Knights

Technique
Acrylic

A young shepherd in the Alp
Mountain-climbing
Entrance to the cave
Sleeping knights

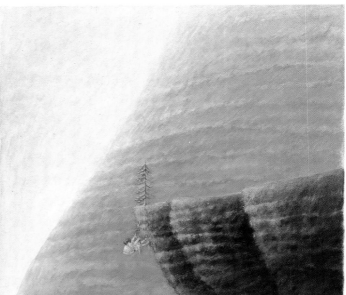

Susanne Bohdal-Lang

Address
Linzerstraße 446
1140 Wien (Austria)

Place and date of birth
Wien, 17 June 1951

Art School attended
Institute of Applied Arts, Vienna

Works published by
Nord-Süd Verlag/Mönchaltorf

Title of the work
Under the Gingkotree

Technique
Pencil

Albinoni, the Gingkomidget
Antonia
Antonia meets Albinoni
At the end of the long voyage...

Silke Brix-Henker

Address
Bahrenfelder Steindamm 89
2000 Hamburg 50
(Federal Republic of Germany)

Place and date of birth
Probsteierhagen, 28 February 1951

Art School attended
Institute of Applied Arts, Hamburg

Works published by
Loewes Verlag/Bindlach
Annette Betz Verlag/Wien

Title of the work
Kasimir Must Not Crow

Publisher and date of publication
Annette Betz Verlag, 1986

Technique
Watercolour

Kate discovers Kasimir
A cock like Kasimir
The cock ought to be banned
Kasimir must not crow
Peace at last

Marie-Claude Cadillon

Address
Cité Dorat, 55F Rue Durcy
33130 Begles (France)

Place and date of birth
Libourne, 8 March 1950

Works published by
S'Editions / Laroin

Title of the work
Portraits for a Tear-Off Calendar

Technique
Coloured pencils

Isidore
The sun

Eric Carle

Address
West Hill Road
Charlemont MA 01339 (USA)

Date of birth
1929

Art School attended
Academy of Applied Arts, Stuttgart

Works published by
Picture Book Studio/London,
Boston

Title of the work
All Around Us

Publisher and date of publication
Picture Book Studio, 1986

Manuel Castellanos

Address
Viljelijäntie 4-6 A6
00410 Helsinki (Finland)

Place and date of birth
Sancti Spiritus (Cuba), 29 May 1949

Art School attended
National School of Arts, Cubanacán
(Havana)

Works published by
Casa de las Americas/Havana
Gente Nueva/Havana
Letras Cubanas/Havana
Love-Kirja/Helsinki
Weilin + Göös/Helsinki

Title of the work
Orunla and the Turtle's Drum

Publisher and date of publication
Weilin + Göös, 1986

Technique
Coloured pencils, watercolours and
gold colours (mixed technique)

Prince Aremo disobeying the orders
of Orunla, the god of divination
In less than no time, the slow turtle
plunged into the river in order to
save the prince
The turtle closed his precious slave
inside the drum
Orunla helped the boy out of the
drum and put an echo in his place
Deep in his heart the king was not
able to enjoy the animated and
colourful celebration

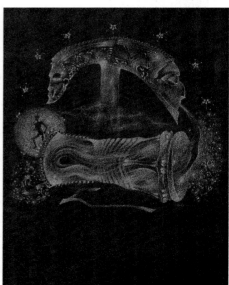

Alberto Celletti

Address
Via Monte dei 9 Draghi 22
00144 Roma (Italy)

Place and date of birth
Viterbo, 2 March 1964

Art School attended
European Institute of Design, Rome

Title of the work
A Strange Kind of War

Technique
Watercolour with coloured pencils

Prisoner in the country of soap-
bubbles
Sabotage!

Pierre Cornuel

Address
4 Rue de la République
78100 Saint Germain en Laye
(France)

Place and date of birth
Chantenay Villedieu (Sarthe),
28 October 1952

Art School attended
ESAM

Works published by
Editions Nathan/Paris

Title of the work
The Town Mouse, the Country
Mouse

Publisher and date of publication
Nathan, 1987

Technique
Watercolour and sepia ink

Scrambling up to the larder
The country mouse returns home
Walking in the country, they pick
flowers

André Dahan

Address
18 Rue du Moulin de la Vierge
75014 Paris (France)

Place and date of birth
Algiers, 2 May 1935

Art School attended
Decorative Arts, Paris

Works published by
Editions Gallimard/Paris
Vif Argent/Neuilly-sur-Seine
Librairie Hatier/Paris
Bayard Presse/Paris
Alibaba Verlag/Frankfurt
Viking Penguin/New York
Penguin/London
Bohem Press/Zurich

Title of the work
My Friend the Moon

Technique
Oil on paper

Why, hello Moon
I just happened to be passing by
Uh oh
Oh my, can you swim!
Let me help you

André Dahan
© 1986

Rolf De Bruin

Address
v.d. Broekelaan 18
1185 DA Amstelveen
(The Netherlands)

Place and date of birth
Amsterdam, 27 March 1956

Works published by
Sjaloom/Utrecht
W.J. Wildeboer/Haarlem
Van Goor/Amsterdam
Wereldbibliotheek/Amsterdam

Title of the work
The Edge of the Rainbow

Technique
Pencil and ink

Little chap thinks about his
feelings
The staircase at the beginning of the
rainbow fades
Little chap starts his quest for the
rainbow
Little chap first sees the rainbow
The staircase at the foot of the
rainbow fades

Marino Degano

Address
*5 Rue de Bâle
67100 Strasbourg (France)*

Place and date of birth
Udine (Italy), 22 June 1960

Art School attended
*School of Decorative Arts,
Strasbourg*

Works published by
*Lito/Paris
Glénat/Grenoble
Milan/Toulose*

Title of the work
Hot Dragons

Publisher and date of publication
Editions Glénat, 1986

Technique
Coloured inks (ecoline)

*The rainbow
A dragon in the snow*

Valeria Della Valentina

Address
Via Carducci 12
33077 Sacile PN (Italy)

Place and date of birth
Sacile, 10 October 1961

Art Schools attended
Art School, Pordenone
Academy of Fine Arts, Venice

Title of the work
Who Knows Where Rainbows Come
From?

Technique
Mixed media

After a storm there is always a
rainbow
Colours, more colours!

Angelo Di Garbo

Address
Via Giovanni di Cristina 10
90134 Palermo (Italy)

Place and date of birth
Palermo, 25 November 1957

Art Schools attended
Institute of Applied Arts (décor)
Academy of Fine Arts (décor)

Title of the work
The Slow Agony of Via Palazzo
Bruciato

Technique
Etching

Flooding in Via Palazzo Bruciato
Roofs torn off in Via Palazzo
Bruciato
View of Poor Devils' house
The carelessness of Via Palazzo
Bruciato
Fire in Via Palazzo Bruciato

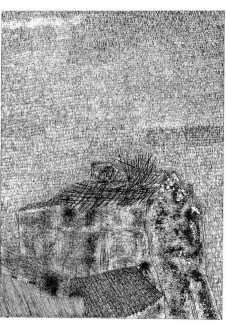

Krystyna Dworak

Address
Daleka 8 m. 3º 77
02024 Warszawa (Poland)

Place and date of birth
Cracovia, 23 April 1938

Art School attended
Academy of Arts, Warsaw

Title of the work
Adventures of Sinbad the Sailor

Technique
Gouache, China, Pastels

*Thay day I set out on horseback
from Bagdad to Balsora
A sunny morning sky shone above
me as I was returning home
That day I was in Balsora and the
next day a ship carried me across the
sea to unknown lands
One day our ship was near an
unknown island
A Persian merchant, evidently
anxious, accompanied me when I
returned home*

42

Malgorzata Dzierzawska

Address
13 Rue Van Elewyck
1050 Brussels (Belgium)

Place and date of birth
Warsaw (Poland), 9 April 1955

Art School attended
Institute of Architecture and Visual
Arts, Brussels

Works published by
Casterman/Tournai
Bayard-Presse/Paris
Fernand Nathan/Paris

Title of the work
Animal Stories

Publisher and date of publication
Fernand Nathan, 1986

Technique
Pencil

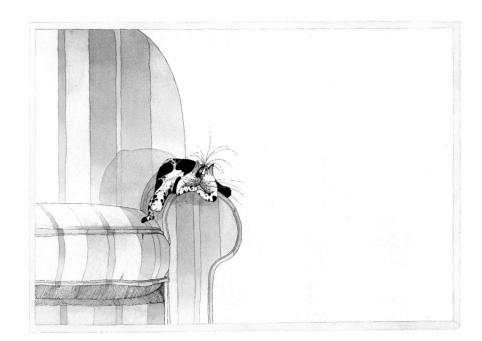

Pablo Echevarria

Address
Pedro de Valdivia 4 4º
28006 Madrid (Spain)

Place and date of birth
Bilbao, 26 March 1963

Works published by
Ediciones S.M. / Madrid

Title of the work
Popoty

Technique
Watercolour and ink

Popoty in the armchair
Twelfth-cake
Ms. Pelucona dancing
Time for breakfast

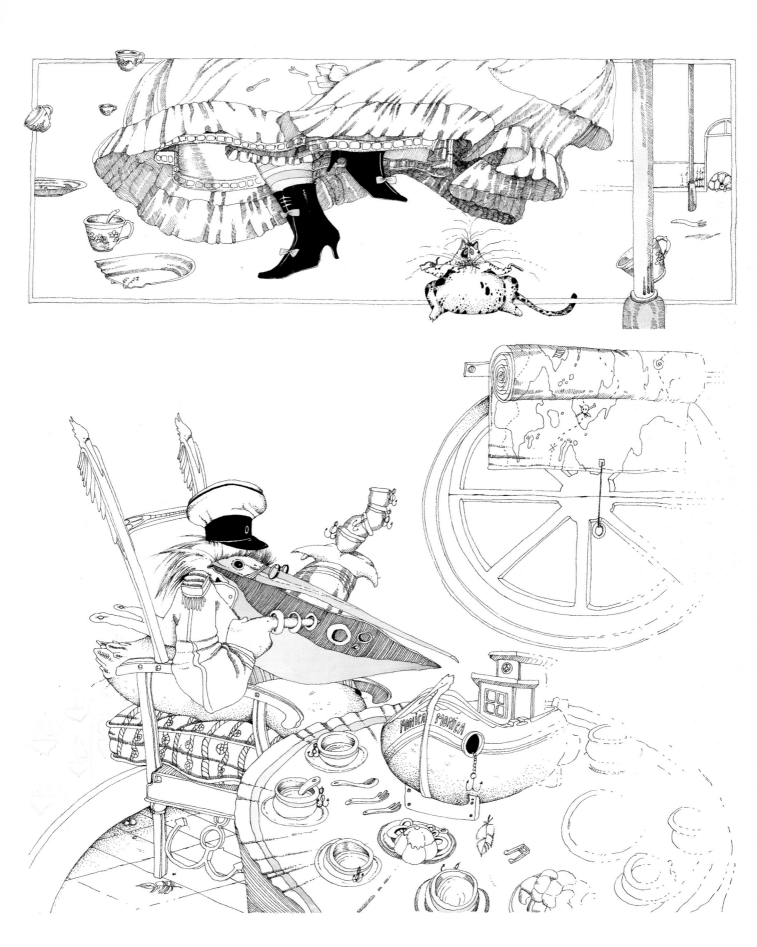

Elisabetta Franco

Address
Via Antonino Pio 75
00145 Roma (Italy)

Date of birth
1 July 1925

Art School attended
State School of Art, Urbino

Works published by
Edizioni Paoline/ Roma

Title of the work
The Four Seasons

Technique
Watercolour

Spring
Summer
Autumn
Winter
Autumn fruit

E. Franco '86

Antonio Frasconi

Address
26 Dock Road
South Norwalk CT 06854 (USA)

Place and date of birth
Montevideo (Uruguay), 28 April 1919

Title of the work
The World Upside Down

Technique
Woodcuts

Caged
Butcher
Circus
Doghouse
Orders

Danièle Friedrich

Address
*30, Route de Mittelhausbergen
67200 Strasbourg (France)*

Place and date of birth
Strasbourg, 10 May 1960

Art School attended
*Institute of Decorative Arts,
Strasbourg*

Works published by
*Neugebauer Press / Salzburg,
Munich
Picture Book Studio / London,
Boston*

Title of the work
The Brown Elmtree

Technique
Watercolour and pen

Jesús Gabán Bravo

Address
Urb. Montenebros 7
28400 Villalba-Madrid (Spain)

Place and date of birth
Madrid, 10 January 1957

Art School attended
Institute of Fine Arts, Madrid

Works published by
Ediciones Altea/Madrid
Ediciones Miñon/Valladolid
Ediciones Destino/Barcelona
Ediciones La Galera/Barcelona
Editorial Argos Vergara/Barcelona
Ediciones S.M./Madrid
Larousse/Paris
Gakken/Tokyo

Title of the work
Alfanhuí

Technique
Mixed

The whole room was full of birds...
Its four legs had grown roots
He made room for me on the stone...
Alfanhuí sat down and looked at
Faulo...
In the next curve the snake strung
the second ring

Ivan Gantschev

Address
Bettinastraße 33
6000 Frankfurt 1
(Federal Republic of Germany)

Place and date of birth
Tirnovo (Bulgaria), 4 January 1925

Art School attended
Academy of Fine Arts, Sofia

Works published by
Picture Book Studio / London,
Boston
Neugebauer Press / Salzburg,
Munich
Gakken / Tokyo
Bohem Press / Zurich

Title of the work
Canoeing

Technique
Watercolour

Mensadik Garipov

Place and date of birth
Ustinov (USSR), 1946

Art School attended
Polygraphic Institute, Moscow

Title of the work
Tales from Udmurtia

Technique
Etching

Willi Glasauer

Address
Rue Vira
66220 St. Paul de Fenouillet (France)

Place and date of birth
Stříbro (Czechoslovakia),
9 December 1938

Art School attended
Art School, Mayence

Works published by
L'Ecole des loisirs / Paris
Editions Gallimard / Paris
Sauerländer / Aarau
Dumont Verlag / Köln
Beltz & Gelberg / Weinheim

Title of the work
The Chess King's Return

Publisher and date of publication
Verlag Sauerländer, 1986

Technique
Pigment type ink

The downunder
The upperhigher
The aboveover
The Chess King's reception
In an empty tower

Can Göknil

Address
Ayse Sultan Korusu,
Ciftciler Apt. 10/5
Bebek 80810 Istanbul (Turkey)

Place and date of birth
Ankara, 3 August 1945

Art Schools attended
Knox College, Galesburg
The City College, New York

Works published by
Redhouse Press/Istanbul
Verlag Yvonne Landeck/Frankfurt
Dag Yeli Verlag/Frankfurt
Beltz Verlag/Weinheim

Title of the work
The porcupine story

Technique
Watercolour

It rained and rained. The animals
were grateful to the porcupine for
helping them
Ever since then, the porcupine has
had many friends

Bob Graham

Address
Lot 8 Main Road
Mount Dandenong 3767 Victoria
(Australia)

Place and date of birth
Sydney, 20 October 1942

Art School attended
Julian Ashton Art School, Sydney

Works published by
William Collins / Sydney
Thomas Lothian / Port Melbourne
The Five Mile Press / Hawthorn
Omnibus Books / Adelaide
Bayard Press / Paris
Hamish Hamilton / London
Walker Books / London

Title of the work
The Wild

Publisher and date of publication
Thomas Lothian, 1986

Technique
Inks, crayon and watercolour

Deep in the forest it is still and quiet.
There are places with the smell of
foxes, and places that drip. The
children look for their pets
everywhere

Yasuyuki Hamamoto

Address
20-402 Momoyama-jutaku,
165 Momoyama-1-chome, Midori-ku,
Nagoya 458 (Japan)

Place and date of birth
Nagoya, 12 January 1955

Title of the work
A boat in the field

Technique
Acrylic colours, coloured pencils

Haru resting. He does not notice the
fierce eagles
Haru sees three thieves running
away
Suddenly whales appear
Haru finds a boat in the field
Haru flies over the castle

Yoko Handa

Address
2-6 Shirayuki Shataku,
5-12, Itami 4-chome, Itami-shi,
Hyogo-ken (Japan)

Place and date of birth
Hyogo-ken, 1 January 1951

Title of the work
Yukiwatari (by Miyazawa Kenji)

Technique
Watercolour, Japanese paper

Silently falling snow, suddenly falling snow, the field's bean-filled buns are hot-puff, puff, puff. Tauemon, the wandering drunk had 38 last year.
Silently falling snow, suddenly falling snow, the field's moodles are laughing-ho, ho, ho. Kiyosaku, the wandering drunk ate 13 last year. Kick, kick, tap, tap. Kick, kick, tap, tap.
Kick, kick, kick, kick, tap, tap, tap. Fox yelp, little fox. Konbei the fox caught his left leg in a trap last year, yelp, yelp, rattle, rattle, yelp, yelp, yelp.
Fox yelp, little fox. Konsuke the fox tried to steal a fried fish, and his tail caught on fire, yap, yap, yap.

«There's a fox slide show tonight, do you wanna go?»
«Let's go. Let's go. Fox, yelp, little fox, fox yelp Konsaburo»

68

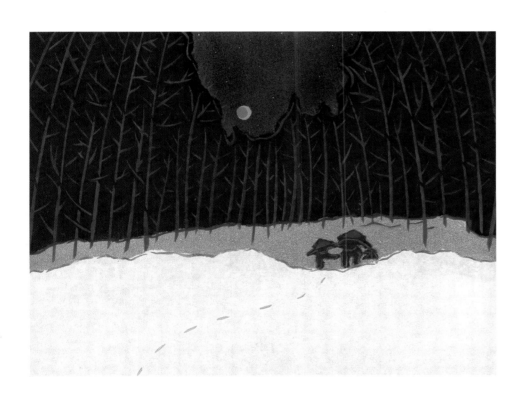

Helme Heine

Address
Viktoriastraße 2
8000 München 40
(Federal Republic of Germany)

Place and date of birth
Berlin, 4 April 1941

Works published by
Middelhauve / Köln

Technique
Watercolour, pen

Toyokuni Honda

Address
1-2-6 Kamidaira Fussa-shi
Tokyo (Japan)

Place and date of birth
Shibuya (Tokyo), 31 August 1945

Art School attended
Nippon Design School, Tokyo

Title of the work
A Tale of an Old Man Who Lost his Lump

Technique
Lino cut and watercolour

Once upon a time there was a joyful old man who had a huge, ugly lump on his cheeck
Dawn is breaking. The old man says good-bye and the ogres say «Hey, grand-pa, you must come and show us your dance tomorrow night again. To make sure you don't break the promise, we will keep your big lump here»

72

Rachel Isadora

Address
229¹/₂ East 81st Street, Apt. 3R
New York NY 10028 (USA)

Place and date of birth
New York, 27 October 1952

Works published by
Greenwill/New York
Dial Books/New York

Title of the work
Flossie and the Fox

Publisher and date of publication
Dial Books, 1986

Technique
Pencil, black ink, watercolour

Etienne Jung

Address
25 Route du Marienbronn
67250 Lobsann (France)

Place and date of birth
Wissenbourg, 14 April 1964

Art School attended
School of Decorative Arts,
Strasbourg

Title of the work
Crab Apple

Technique
Coloured inks and black pastel

«That's too much for me»
The first flying lesson
He didn't understand, yet

76

Steven Kellogg

Address
Bennetts Bridge Road
Sandy Hook CT 06842 (USA)

Date of birth
26 October 1941

Art School attended
School of Design, Rhode Island

Works published by
William Morrow/New York

Title of the work
Pecos Bill (American Tall Tale)

Publisher and date of publication
William Morrow, 1986

Technique
Mixed Watercolour, inks, acrylic

In pioneering days when Pecos Bill
was a baby his family piled into
covered wagons and headed west

Ute Krause

Address
Nehringstraße 21/22 (Hinterhaus)
1000 Berlin 19
(Federal Republic of Germany)

Place and date of birth
Berlin, 19 December 1960

Art School attended
Institute of Arts, Berlin

Works published by
Middelhauve/Köln

Title of the work
The Santa Klaus Men

Publisher and date of publication
Middelhauve, 1985

Technique
Watercolour

Kurtchen finds the Santa postcard
Big celebration at the Santa home

Zdenka Krejčová

Address
Slavíčkova 1/361
160 00 Praha 6 (Czechoslovakia)

Place and date of birth
Prague, 3 November 1944

Art Schools attended
Atelier Prof. Svolinský, Prague
Arts and Crafts College, Prague

Works published by
Artia/Prague
Albatros/Prague
Odeon/Prague

Title of the work
Fairytales from Vietnam

Technique
Paintings on silk

The Wise Monkeys
The Fish-scale Fairy
God of the Long Age
The Man and the Demon

Josef Kremláček

Address
Okrajová 1071
67401 Třebíč (Czechoslovakia)

Place and date of birth
Třebíč, 5 March 1937

Art School attended
School of Art, Prague

Works published by
Artia/Prague

Title of the work
Legends and tales of the Pharaohs

Publisher and date of publication
Artia, 1985

Technique
Mixed

Michèle Lemieux

Address
5155 Rue de Bordeaux
Montreal H2H 2A6 (Canada)

Place and date of birth
Quebec, 29 May 1955

Art School attended
School of Visual Arts, Quebec

Works published by
Otto Maier Verlag/Ravensburg
William Morrow/New York
Gakken/Tokyo
Methuen/London

Title of the work
Amahl and the Night Visitors

Publisher and date of publication
William Morrow, 1986

Technique
Watercolour

From far away we come, and further
we must go. How far, how far, my
crystal star
At the window, Amahl watched as a
magnificent caravan approached his
house
King Melchior
Amahl, with his crutch still raised,
took a step forward

Maria Cristina Malaquias

Address
*Av. Das Tílias, Viv. Cândida
Rinchôa 2735 Cacém (Portugal)*

Place and date of birth
Queluz, 15 August 1955

Art School attended
Visual Art & Communication Centre

Works published by
*Castoliva Editora/Porto
Livros Horizonte/Lisboa
Editora Comunicação/Lisboa
Texto Editora/Lisboa
Plátano Editora/Lisboa*

Title of the work
The black sheep

Technique
Pastel, coloured pencils and gouache

*The sun was about to rise, and the
sky was filled with white clouds
Looking closely they had little faces
with eyes and everything
They unrolled themselves and came
down slowly, as if they had
parachutes
After all they were just hungry...
It was the end of the story (or so it
seemed) when suddenly in the middle
of a great noise it finally fell... the
black sheep*

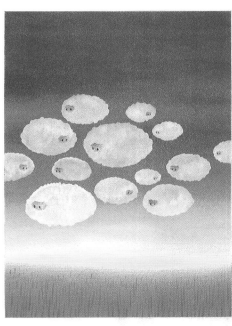

Lorella Manenti

Address
Via Trieste 14
24064 Grumello del Monte BG (Italy)

Place and date of birth
Bergamo, 7 February 1961

Art School attended
Cartoonists College, Milan

Title of the work
Memoirs of a Rogue (by Sergej
Esemin)

Technique
Mixed

The poet
The tree and the eggs
The rogue
The horse
Twilight

Alan Marks

Address
9 Selbridge Ct. Prince's Road
Wimbledon SW19 (Great Britain)

Art Schools attended
College of Art and Design, Medway
Academy of Art, Bath

Works published by
Heinemann/London
Hamish Hamilton/London

Title of the work
Nowhere to be found

Technique
Mixed media

Don't stray beyond the arches where
the lost children play
...and heard the lost children
chanting
Inside the shop sat a kindly woman
knitting frantically

Jiřina Marton

Address
5 Cowan Avenue
Toronto, Ontario M6K 2N1
(Canada)

Place and date of birth
Liberec (Czechoslovakia),
19 April 1946

Art School attended
School of Applied Arts, Prague

Works published by
Editions Lito/Champigny-s/M
Bohem Press/Zurich
Gakken/Tokyo
Annick Press/Toronto

Title of the work
Nicole's boat

Technique
Acrylic

Nicole was sailing away to the end of the day, down the long winding river that goes to the sea
Nicole and the crow went sailing away...
Nicole, the crow and the cow went sailing away...
Nicole, the crow, the cow and the kittens went sailing away...
...so ride the right waves as you brave the night sea

Shinobu Matsui

Address
Takatsukasa 4-4-7, 1-404
Takarazuka-Shi, Hyogo (Japan)

Place and date of birth
Hyogo, 31 January 1957

Title of the work
With the «Star»

Technique
Acrylic

Hotel (can you have a dream?)
Ocean (a whale carried the «star» in
a moonlight ocean)

Capucine Mazille

Address
Orbessy-Bas St. Eusebe
74150 Rumilly (France)

Place and date of birth
The Hague (Netherlands),
23 December 1953

Art School attended
Royal Academy of Art, The Hague

Title of the work
The Hobbit

Technique
Watercolour

In the pinetree
The dragon

98

Yoshi Miyazaki

Address
*P.O. Box 353 Warner Hill Road
Charlemont MA 01339 (USA)*

Place and date of birth
Japan, 23 March 1943

Art School attended
University of Art, Tokyo

Works published by
*Picture Book Studio/London,
Boston*

Raffaello Mori

Address
Via della Chiesa 73
50125 Firenze (Italy)

Place and date of birth
Reggello (Florence), 27 March 1934

Title of the work
Jonathan Livingston Seagull

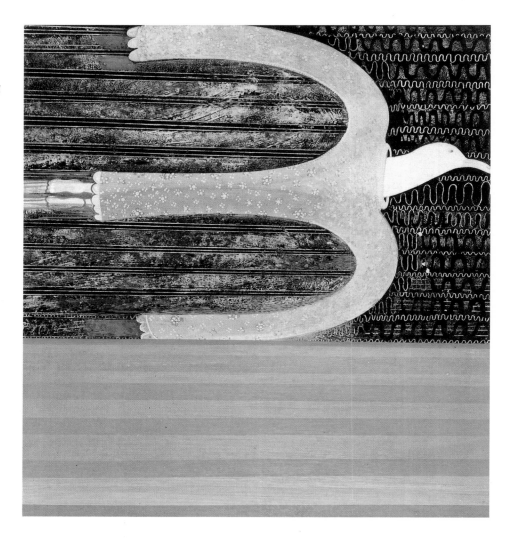

Junko Morimoto

Address
16-786 Military Road
Mosman, NSW 2088 (Australia)

Place and date of birth
Hiroshima (Japan), 31 March 1931

Art School attended
University of Art, Kyoto

Works published by
William Collins/Sydney
Lothian/Melbourne

Title of the work
Kojuro and the Bears

Publisher and date of publication
William Collins Australia, 1986

Technique
Watercolour, ink, pencil, air brush
etc. on paper

«I'm sure it's snow, Mother»,
said the cub
«Forgive me, Kojuro. I don't
hate you but the choice isn't mine»
Mt. Nametoko; rushing down its
side are the Ozora Falls, and it was
here that the famous bear of Mt.
Nametoko once lived
Kojuro was a hunter not because he
wanted to be, but for him there was
no other choice

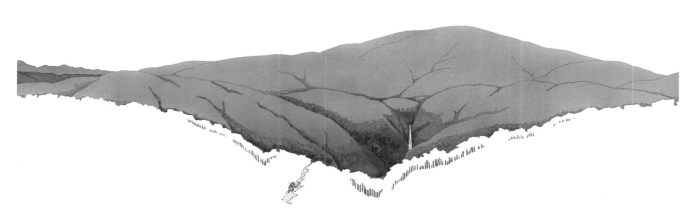

Chantal Muller van den Berghe

Address
49 Rue de la Mairie
67200 Wolfisheim (France)

Place and date of birth
Roubaix, 13 October 1936

Art Schools attended
School of Fine Arts, Tourcoing
School of Decorative Arts,
Strasbourg
Arts Association, Princeton

Works published by
Hatier / Paris
Grasset et Fasquelle / Paris
Nord-Süd Verlag / Zurich
Bohem Press / Zurich
Gakken / Tokyo

Title of the work
Sebastian, Top of the Class

Publisher and date of publication
Nord-Süd Verlag, 1986

Technique
Coloured inks

Once, I came in a giant baloon,
decorated with flowers
And also on the back of a great and
very soft bird
Once I got caught on the ribbon of a
kite
Once again it was in a real plane I
went up, with four motors

106

Erik Hjorth Nielsen

Address
Spergelmarken 17
2860 Søborg-Kobenhavn (Denmark)

Place and date of birth
Copenhagen, 13 July 1937

Art School attended
Royal Academy of Fine Arts,
Copenhagen

Works published by
Gyldendal/Copenhagen

Title of the work
The Troll from Wolff Mountain

The troll tests the boy
Through the sinister forest

108

Bernhard Oberdieck

Address
Schloß Zellerreit
8091 Ramerberg
(Federal Republic of Germany)

Place and date of birth
Oerlinghausen, 24 February 1949

Art School attended
Institute of Applied Arts, Bielefeld

Works published by
Ars Edition / Munich
Ellermann Verlag / Munich
DTV-Junior / Munich
Fabula Verlag / Bad Aibling
Loewes Verlag / Bindlach
Arena Verlag / Würzburg
Oberon BV / Haarlem
Thienemanns Verlag / Stuttgart

Title of the work
The Earth is Your Home, the Sky a Window - Since the Beginning of the World

Publisher and date of publication
Ars Edition, 1986

Technique
Coloured pencil, crayon

Reptiles, insects and flowers conquered the world
There are different birds
The animals sleep, watchful

Rosario Oliva

Address
Via Piave 2
80126 Napoli (Italy)

Place and date of birth
Napoli, 4 May 1965

Art Schools attended
State School of Art, Naples
The European Institute of Design,
Rome

Title of the work
Reflexes

Technique
Watercolour

The slothful reflex
The playful reflex
The joker reflex
The absent reflex
The spiteful reflex

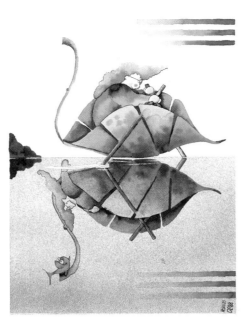

Carme Peris

Address
Avgda. Republica Argentina 261
08000 Barcelona (Spain)

Place and date of birth
Barcelona, 30 November 1941

Art School attended
School of Arts and Crafts, Barcelona

Works published by
La Galera/Barcelona
Ediciones Hymsa/Barcelona
Ediciones Proa/Barcelona
Gakken/Japan
Silver Burdett/USA
Castermann/Tournai

Title of the work
Canigo (by Jacint Verdaguer)

Technique
Acrylic

Moors landing in Cotlliure
Before being knighted, Gentil keeps
watch over the arms

114

Marcus Pfister

Address
Bümplizstrasse 109
3018 Bern (Switzerland)

Place and date of birth
Bern, 30 July 1960

Art School attended
School of Arts and Crafts, Bern

Works published by
Nord-Süd Verlag / Mönchaltorf

Title of the work
Four Candles for Simon

Publisher and date of publication
Nord-Süd Verlag, 1986

Technique
Mixed watercolour and pastel

Simon reaches his sheep
Two shepherds in Galilea

Christian Pieroni

Address
2 Montée St. Eloi
83330 Le Castellet (France)

Place and date of birth
Marseilles, 9 June 1949

Art School attended
*Luminy School of Fine Arts,
Marseilles*

Works published by
La Farandole / Paris
Editions de l'amitié / Paris
Bayard Press / Paris
Editions de Seuil / Paris
Ars Editions / Munich

Title of the work
The Magic Key

Technique
Ink and pencil

The voyage across the sea
The run after the bird

Paola Poli

Address
Via Bolognese 77
50139 Firenze (Italy)

Place and date of birth
Florence, 25 June 1966

Art School attended
Course in painting

Title of the work
Book of Illustrations for Fables

Technique
Mixed technique

Anke Prahl

Address
Löfflerstraße 25
2000 Hamburg 50
(Federal Republic of Germany)

Place and date of birth
Hamburg, 21 March 1959

Art School attended
School of Applied Arts, Hamburg

Works published by
Loewes Verlag/Bindlach

Title of the work
Cloak of Feathers (by Christa König)

Publisher and date of publication
Loewes Verlag, 1986

Technique
Pen, ink

An enormous cloud of birds is
swarming in the air above the tower
She has just freed several thrushes,
when the man from the castle
appears

František Procházka

Address
Palackého 281/23
250 88 Čelákovice n./Lab.
(Czechoslovakia)

Place and date of birth
Přerov na Moravě, 11 June 1911

Art School attended
Academy of Applied Arts, Prague

Title of the work
Our Mushrooms and Plants Known
and Unknown

Technique
Watercolour and pastel

Solanum melongena
Malus silvestris
Nymphalis xanthomelas

Olga Ptackova

Address
Slovenska 23
Praha (Czechoslovakia)

Place and date of birth
Staskov, 23 August 1955

Art School attended
Academy of Arts, Prague

Title of the work
Kalevala (Finnish epic)

Technique
Mixed

Daniel Rabanal

Address
Uruguay 1034
Buenos Aires 1016 (Argentina)

Place and date of birth
Buenos Aires, 9 July 1949

Works published by
Hyspamerica / Buenos Aires
Ediciones La Urraca / Buenos Aires

Title of the work
An armchair, for instance

Technique
Pen, ink, colour and pencil

An armchair is a step
For you to sit and tell me a tale,
about a funny traveller who
wandered practically everywhere
and never left his armchair

Mitra Reyhani Gadim

Address
Insirah Bebek Sok. No: 41/4
80810 Istanbul (Turkey)

Place and date of birth
Tehran (Iran), 10 July 1966

Art School attended
Istanbul Art School (first year)

Works published by
Red House/Istanbul

Title of the work
Little Red Riding Hood

Technique
Gouache

He sprang on the old lady and
devoured her in a twinkling, since he
had had nothing to eat for over three
days
«Does she live far from here?» asked
the wolf
As she was going through a wood...

Josefina Rifà

Address
c/Mallorca 545 1er.
08000 Barcelona (Spain)

Place and date of birth
Palma de Mallorca, 21 July 1939

Art School attended
School of Fine Arts, Barcelona

Works published by
Editorial Casals/Barcelona
Editorial Onda/Barcelona
Edebè/Barcelona
La Galera Editorial/Barcelona
Ediciones de la Magrana/Barcelona
Abadia de Montserrat/Barcelona
Editorial Cuïlla/Barcelona
Editorial Juventud/Barcelona
Ediciones Proa/Barcelona

Title of the work
The adventures of Ulysses

Technique
Watercolour

The Syrens call Ulysses who ignores
the danger
Trojan horse

Susanne Riha

Address
Hafnergasse 5/11
Wien (Austria)

Place and date of birth
Vienna, 18 June 1954

Art School attended
School of Graphic Design, Vienna

Works published by
Annette Betz Verlag/Vienna
Jugend und Volk/Vienna

Title of the work
The Year

Technique
Gouache

January
September
October
December

Lorella Rizzatti

Address
Via Ranuzzi 28
44040 Casaglia FE (Italy)

Place and date of birth
Ferrara, 6 September 1963

Art School attended
Institute of Art, Ferrara

Title of the work
Bee Bombo's Friends

Technique
Watercolour, coloured inks

Sylvia, the little bird, on the thorn-
bush
Camomilla, the daisy, on the lawn
Sophie, the snail, by the stream
Philip, the rabbit, in the grass

Marie-José Sacré

Address
18 Rue Bertholet Deschamps
4880 Spa (Belgium)

Place and date of birth
Battice, 4 August 1946

Art School attended
Academy of Fine Arts, Liège

Works published by
Bohem Press/Zurich
Editions Duculot/Gembloux
Casterman/Tournai
H. Dessain/Liège
Gakken/Tokyo
Atelier Muze/Siki-Shi

Title of the work
Bon Appetit, Mister Ogre

Publisher and date of publication
H. Dessain, 1986

Technique
Watercolour

At the grocer's
Mister Ogre waiting for the bus

138

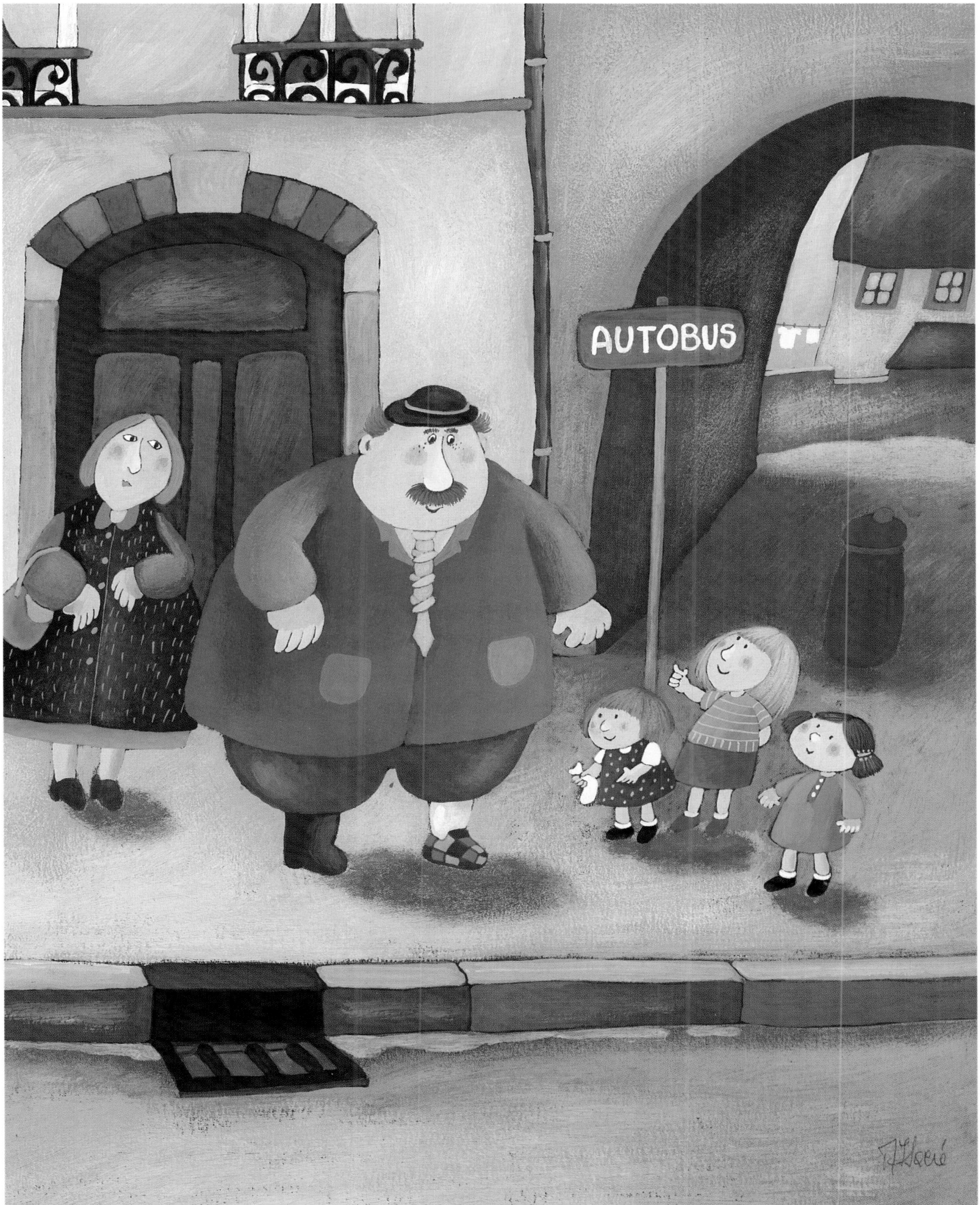
AUTOBUS

Francesca Salucci

Address
Via Montaletto 30
47042 Cesenatico FO (Italy)

Place and date of birth
Bassano del Grappa,
9 October 1969

Art School attended
State School of Animation, Urbino

Title of the work
The Mystery of the Old Wood

Technique
Watercolour washes

The five nightmares that visit
Benvenuto
Colonel Procolo is told off by his own
shadow
The secret conversation between
Colonel Procolo and the genius
Bernardi
The wind, Matteo, greets Benvenuto
on the mountain

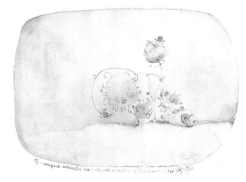

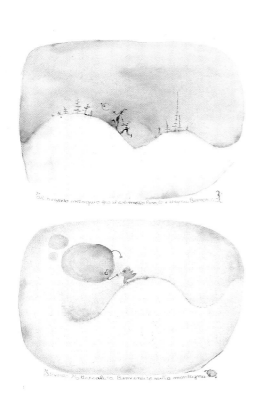

Bel neonato rotolava giù si dimena finché a terra Benvenuto 3

Benvenuto Benvenuto Benvenuto sulla montagna

Aleksej Schmarinov

Place and date of birth
Moskva (USSR), 1933

Art School attended
Art Institute, Moscow

Works published by
*Nudojestvennaja
Literatura/Moscow
Detskaja Literatura/Moscow*

*Title of the work
Illustrations to Poems by Rustaveli*

Technique
Etching

Renate Seelig

Address
Roederbergweg 39
6000 Frankfurt 1
(Federal Republic of Germany)

Place and date of birth
Bielefeld, 29 May 1938

Art School attended
High School of Arts, Hamburg

Works published by
Ellermann Verlag/Munich

Title of the work
The Singing, Soaring Lark

Publisher and date of publication
Ellermann Verlag, 1986

Technique
Ink and coloured pencil

He dreamt he heard the pine trees
rustling
Everything has been a bad dream

Brigitte Smith

Address
Odinstraße 29
8000 München 81
(Federal Republic of Germany)

Place and date of birth
Stalp, 26 June 1938

Art Schools attended
School of Arts and Crafts,
Wiesbaden
Academy of Graphic Art, Munich
Academy of Fine Arts, Montreal

Works published by
Dial Books/New York
Scribner's Sons/New York
Macmillan/New York
Benziger/Zurich
Parabel/Zurich
Bitter Verlag/Recklinghausen
Schneider Verlag/Munich
Schwann Verlag/Düsseldorf
Arena Verlag/Würzburg
Hoch Verlag/Düsseldorf
Deutscher Taschenbuch
Verlag/Munich
Tafelberg Publishers/Cape Town

Title of the work
When Witches are Bewitching

Technique
Watercolour

Introduction to characters
House of witch «Kobeia»
Kobeia's attempt

Carme Solé Vendrell

Address
Sant Alexandre 54 at. 3º
08031 Barcelona (Spain)

Place and date of birth
Barcelona, 1 August 1944

Art School attended
School of Arts and Crafts, Massana

Works published by
Ediciones Destino/Barcelona
Ediciones Hymsa/Barcelona
Editorial La Galera/Barcelona
Parramon Ediciones/Barcelona
Casals/Barcelona
Ediciones Altea/Madrid
Miñon/Valladolid
Bayard Press/Paris
Grasset et Fasquelle/Paris
Centurion Jeunesse/Paris
Blackie & Son/London
Andersen Press/London
Schwann Verlag/Düsseldorf
Casterman/Belgium

Title of the work
Night Music

Technique
Mixed

Later, at sunset...

Jutta Soyka

Address
Artzbergweg 6
4030 Ratingen 8
(Federal Republic of Germany)

Place and date of birth
Aschaffenburg, 3 March 1955

Art School attended
Institute for Figurative Arts,
Würzburg

Title of the work
Gnome to Move and Mates in Two

Technique
Watercolour, coloured pencils

What the hell did Ratzparow move,
Vienna 1958?
The poisoned pawn
To clean up the pieces
Chessless time
Chequered dream

Borislav Stoev

Address
Bul. Samokov Bl. 305
Sofia (Bulgaria)

Place and date of birth
Sofia, 21 September 1927

Art School attended
Academy of Fine Arts, Sofia

Works published by
Bulgarski Hudoinik/Sofia
Narodna Mladej/Sofia
Bulgarski Pisatel/Sofia
Sofia Press/Sofia
Gakken/Tokyo
Forja/Lisbon

Title of the work
Book for Boys

Publisher and date of publication
Bulgarski Hudoinik, 1986

Technique
Watercolour, Pencil

Aspasia Surgailene

Place and date of birth
Vilnjus (USSR), 1928

Art School attended
Art Institute of Lithuania

Works published by
Vaga/Vilna

Title of the work
Tales of Giumaitia

Technique
Gouache

Gianluigi Susinno

Address
Sentiero Buzzanello 13
6974 Aldesago (Switzerland)

Place and date of birth
Boudevilliers, 3 March 1963

Art School attended
European Institute of Design, Milan

Works published by
Medlevant/Lugano

Title of the work
The Pal Street Boys

Technique
Watercolour

Pal Street
In front of the school
The raid on the island of the Red
Shirts
Nemecsek, the hero
The war

Hannu Taina

Address
Torkkelinkuja 20 A 3
00500 Helsinki (Finland)

Place and date of birth
Helsinki, 31 March 1941

Art School attended
University of Industrial Arts,
Helsinki

Works published by
Otava Publishing/Helsinki

Title of the work
Mister King

Technique
Watercolour

And the house had a library, its
shelves filled with books that
whispered among themselves
On the doorstep sat a huge furry cat
«I will stay here», decided the cat.
And it settled in to live with the king
In the evening the king and the cat
were to be seen walking along the
seashore

Jan Tammsaar

Place and date of birth
Tallin (USSR), 1928

Art School attended
University of Arts, Estonia

Works published by
Eesti Raamat/Tallin

Title of the work
Life underwater

Technique
Tempera, Gouache

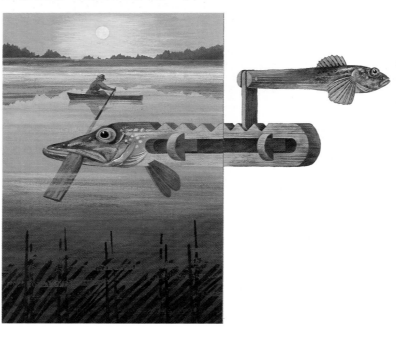

160

Fulvio Testa

Address
Via Leoncino 10
37121 Verona (Italy)

Place and date of birth
Verona, 16 April 1947

Works published by
Abelard-Schumann/London
Andersen Press/London
Ernest Benn/London
Blackie & Son/London
Grisewood & Dempsey/London
Bohem Press/Zurich
J.P. Delarge/Paris
Albin Michel/Paris
Gakken/Tokyo
Hädecke Verlag/Weil der Stadt
Kaufmann/Lahr-Schwarzwald
Nord-Süd Verlag/Mönchaltorf
Patmos/Düsseldorf
Mondadori Ragazzi/Verona
Dial Books/New York
Little, Brown & Co./Boston

Title of the work
Wolf's Favour

Publisher and date of publication
Andersen Press, 1986

Technique
Watercolour, coloured inks, pen and ink

Eve Tharlet

Address
Keréonec
29124 Riec-sur-Belon (France)

Place and date of birth
Mulhouse, 5 July 1956

Art School attended
School of Decorative Arts,
Strasbourg

Works published by
Bayard Presse/Paris
Bordas/Paris
Grasset/Paris
24 Heures Jeunesse/Lausanne
Kaisei-Sha/Tokyo
Gakken/Tokyo
Neugebauer Press/Salzburg,
Munich
Otto Maier Verlag/Ravensburg
Bohem Press/Zurich

Title of the work
Dizzy from Fools

Publisher and plate of publication
Neugebauer Press, 1986

Technique
Watercolour

Nobuhiro Tsusimura

Address
2-4-165 Muicoyama, Takarazuka,
Hyogo-ken (Japan)

Place and date of birth
Osaka, 1938

Art School attended
Art School, Osaka

Works published by
Dainihon Kaiga/Tokyo

Title of the work
Africa, One Day in Africa: Between
the Sky and the Earth

Publisher and date of publication
Dainihon Kaiga, 1986

Technique
Black inks

Morning
Rainbow
Commune
Family

Maria Uszaka

Address
Nowickiego 7/9
Warszawa 02-112 (Poland)

Place and date of birth
Chełm-Lubelski, 30 April 1932

Art School attended
Academy of Art, Warsaw

Works published by
Nasza Księgarnia/Warsaw
Krajowa Agencja
Wydawnicza/Warsaw

Title of the work
Hello, Sunshine (by S. Grabowski)

Publisher and date of publication
Nasza Księgarnia, 1985

Technique
Gouache

A boy in a boat and the ducks
Lady Winter
A faithful dog
Kerosene lamp under an old pear-tree
Geese among the drying sheets

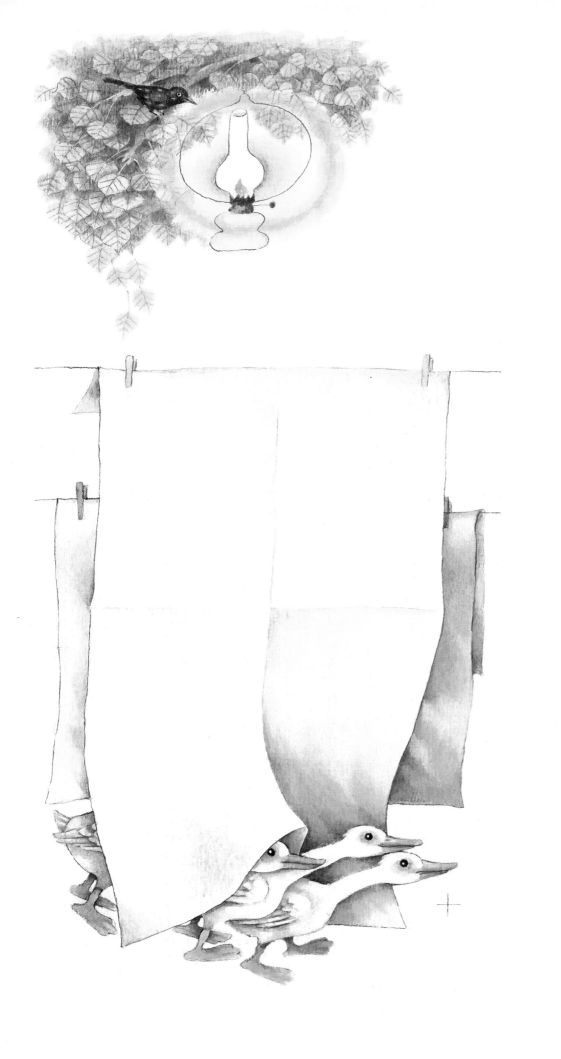

Stefania Vecchi

Address
Piazza Calcagnini D'Este 17
48010 Fusignano RA (Italy)

Place and date of birth
Fusignano, 22 August 1960

Art School attended
Art School
Academy of Fine Arts (Painting)

Title of the work
The Story

Technique
Etching

Anna Vivarés

Address
c/ Atenas 1, 3º2º
08006 Barcelona (Spain)

Art School attended
Llibrer del Mall / Barcelona
Cruïlla / Barcelona
Empurier / Barcelona
Laerter / Barcelona

Title of the work
The Land of the Fools

Technique
Ink, watercolour, coloured pencil

«...and catch the mouse»
«...the rooster»

Aude Weber

Address
75 Boulevard St. Georges
1205 Genève (Switzerland)

Place and date of birth
24 July 1961

Art School attended
School of Decorative Arts, Geneva

Title of the work
The Three Crow Brothers

Technique
China ink

Where the quest begins
The moon's mother
The prince discovers someone hiding
in the tree
The three children come with the
three crow brothers

Andrzej-Ludwik Wloszczynski

Address
Foksal 17 m. 57
00372 Warszawa (Poland)

Place and date of birth
Stawiszyn, 5 July 1951

Art School attended
College of Art, Wrocław

Works published by
Krayowa Agencja
Wydawnicza / Wrocław

Title of the work
Mouse, Cat and Cock (by S.
Trembecki)

Technique
Ink, coloured inks

Mouse
Bombastic tub-thumper and sweet
animal
Cat - a nice animal
Tub-thumper in a yellow boot

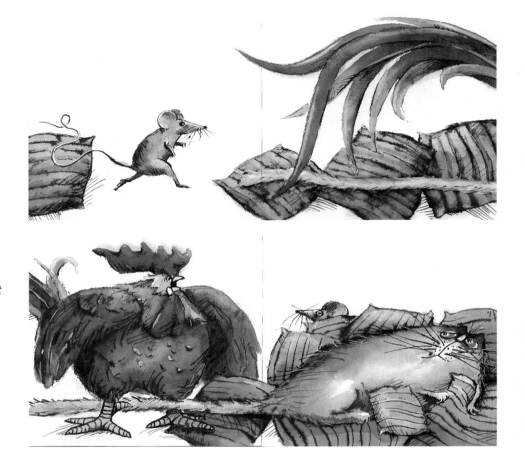

Dita Zak

Address
Kleine Düwelstraße 5
3000 Hannover 1
(Federal Republic of Germany)

Place and date of birth
Holzminden, 4 February 1953

Art School attended
Technical High School, Hildesheim

Works published by
Dragoco-Werke / Holzminden

Title of the work
Brownies

Technique
Watercolour

Sweet dreams
Wiping
Full bath
Breakfast

Lisbeth Zwerger

Place and date of birth
Wien, May 1954

Art School attended
Academy of Applied Art, Vienna

Works published by
Neugebauer Press/Salzburg,
Munich
Picture Book Studio/London,
Boston

Title of the work
The Canterville Ghost

Publisher and date of publication
Neugebauer Press, 1986

Technique
Watercolour

Copyright © 1987
Fiera del Libro per Ragazzi
Piazza Costituzione 6
40128 Bologna, Italy

Co-published with Picture Book Studio
Neugebauer Press
Salzburg, München, London, Boston

Distributed in Italy by
Libreria Parolini
Via Ugo Bassi 14
40121 Bologna, Italy

Distributed in USA by Picture Book Studio,
Natick, MA 01760
Distributed in Canada by Vanwell Publishing,
St. Catherines
Distributed in Australia by Era Publications Ltd.
Adelaide
Distributed by Ragged Bears,
Andover, England

Distributed in all other countries by
Neugebauer Press
Bonauweg 11
5020 Salzburg, Austria